AF428812

# The Poems of my Life

Erika Valles Acosta

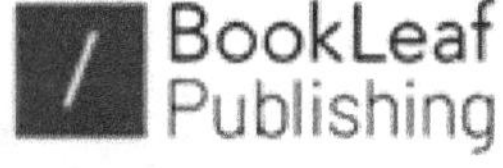

BookLeaf Publishing

The Poems of my Life © 2022 Erika Valles
Acosta

All rights reserved.

No part of this publication may be
reproduced, stored in a retrieval system, or
transmitted, in any form or by any means,
electronic, mechanical, photocopying,
recording or otherwise, without the prior
written permission of the presenters.

Erika Valles Acosta asserts the moral right
to be identified as author of this work.

Presentation by *BookLeaf Publishing*

Web: www.bookleafpub.com

E-mail: info@bookleafpub.com

ISBN: 9789357210942

First edition 2022

# DEDICATION

I thank my family and friends for if it weren't
for them, I would not be here today.

# Five Years

It's been five years, and it still doesn't seem real. How could I go on knowing that this is what's inside me? How can I be me if I know this will change my life? How am I to be a mother when I know this disease has taken over my life? I am not me anymore, I am someone else. I am not me anymore, I am a new person. I am not me anymore, I am just a vessel living inside this body. A body that no longer is functioning. Who am I now? Tell me that. Who am I? Five years, and it's all too real.

# Lost

I am lost. Will I ever be found? All these things inside my head have me spinning round and round. Is this real? Is it fake? How do I know what I am seeing and feeling is the real thing? Will I know, or will I be forever lost? I am lost. SOmeone help me, someone please. I need to know if what I'm seeing is the real thing. Someone save me, someone please. I need to know if what I'm feeling is close to the real thing. I am lost. Will I ever be found?

# Almost

3

I almost ended it all. What do you think that means? I almost gave in. What exactly does that mean? I almost lost my will. How can that be? I almost gave my life, because the pain was too much. Then how am I still alive? I have a great support system, great people behind me. I have a strength I never thought I had. I have everything I could possibly have, yet in the back of my mind I still have that almost. I almost ended it all. Why I survived, is because I rather live for those around me, then be in pain for all eternity.

# Love

Love. What does it mean? Love. Where did it begin? Love. I am fortunate to be with the one I love. I am fortunate to have him in my life. I am fortunate to say that my love for him is strong and his as well. Love makes the world feel so much safer. Love makes me feel I can conquer the world. Love has a funny way of showing people that they truly care for you. And I am fortunate enough to have a man that gives me his all. That is what I think love is. Love is how I feel everyday.

# Life

Life is an opportunity, benefit from it.
Life is beauty, admire it.
Life is bliss, taste ite.
Life is a dream, realize it.
Life is a challenge, meet it.
Life is a duty, complete it.
Life is a game, play it.
Life is a promise, fulfill it.
Life is a song, sing it.
Life is a struggle, accept it.
Life is a tragedy, confront it.
Life is an adventure, dare it.
Life is luck, make it.
Life is precious, do not destroy it.
Life is life, fight for it.

# Listen to my Heart

Listen to my heart, listen to what I have to say. Understand why I'm crying and sighing because you left. Listen to my heart, listen to what I have to say. Understand why I'm leaving you and deceiving you because you left. Listen to my heart, listen to what I have to say. Understand why I'm sharing with you and declaring to you because you left. Listen to my heart, listen to what I have to say. Understand why I'm loving you and touching you because you left. Listen to my heart, listen to what I have to say. Understand why I'm writing to you and talking because all you've been doing is ignoring me and my God.

# Father

I love my father, he doesn't live farther from me.
He can be mean, but it's the only way to
discipline me.
I cry sometimes when he doesn't come home,
but I would die if I found out he was alone.
I care about my father, but I dare not try to be
like him.
No matter what I will always love him, but when
he dies…, no, there is no but.
I will forever love him until I die.

# January 18, 2001

Why did you have to leave me, I've been grieving you. I can't seem to get over you. You died on the 18th of January 2001 and as soon as I heard my father tell my brother, I knew I had become undone. I didn't want to lose you, I wanted to hold onto you tightly. I never got over your death, It's as if a part of me went with you. I had a great relationship with you, but I knew I had to say goodbye. I miss you so much grandpa, and I love you just the same.

# February 18, 2015

I watched you take your last breath, and I must admit it was the most beautiful thing I've ever seen. I watched your beautiful soul leave your body and go to a better place. On that day it was sad, but it was the most gracious and glorious day I could've ever asked for. You gave your son a gift, as well as your grandchildren. TO witness such an empowering moment, I will forever remember. I love you my wonderful grandmother, God has truly gotten the best. May you shine your light upon us whenever possible. We love you.

# Stars that Twinkle

Stars that twinkle every night, I wonder what they say to people who actually look up. Do they tell a story? Does it show you your future? I sleep at night and I dream I'm flying with the stars and I see someone smiling, waving at me. I see he is an elderly man, dark skin, and that distinct black hat. I knew then it was him, my grandfather. I was so happy to see him that I almost flew back to my present life. We went flying and sang a lullaby. I felt at peace with him. I pray every night that I get that chance of seeing him again, but no dream has yet to come. Until then I pray everyday for my grandfather to keep an eye on us. Watch over us. Amen to thee Lord!

# Lighten the Darkness

Lighten the darkness in my heart, set me free so I can fly very far. Let my heart soar high above the clouds and release all worries and doubts. Lighten the darkness in my heart, set me free so I can fly very far. Let me ride the wind at high speed so my hair can flow in peace. Lighten the darkness in my heart, set me free so I can fly very far. Let me roam around in the trees so I can be free from this hell in the world. Lighten the darkness in my heart, set me free so I can fly very far. Let my dreams be with me so I can be a flowing girl. Lighten the darkness in my heart, set me free so I can fly very far.

# What is Love?

What is Love? Love is splendid and wonderful. You can lose yourself, and be in another world. Love has many ways to make you feel special in different ways. It gives you a feel of comfort and serenity. Love is wonderful and awesome, it shows that you have a heart and that you want to care for the person you want to love. Even though love is this, some of these men and women don't have the pleasure to feel love. I used to be that but I believe we all can be loved, we have people who love us. For example, we have our family and friends. Our family will always love us no matter what. Our friends will love and care for us. For we do the same thing for them. So what is love? Love can be anything you want it to be.

# Soulmate

13

I always wondered when I would meet my soulmate. What would he be like? Would he be all that I have asked for? Would he be the kind, and gracious person I have always wanted? How will I know he is my soulmate? When will I know? Someone please tell me. Will they know I am the one for them? Will our eyes meet, and we know then that they are the one? I always wondered when I would meet my soulmate. Will I ever find them? Will my soulmate come?

# I Found Him

14

I found him. Oh God, I found him. I know he's the one. He makes me smile, he makes me laugh, he makes me feel loved like I never felt before. I want him in my life forever, yet how do I do that? I have put up a barrier around my heart for so long that I do not know how to let anyone in. However, he has managed to do just that. My barriers are down and he is in my heart. I have found him. The one that will love me and keep me safe. Forever.

# June 29, 2018

On this day I married the man of my dreams. He proved to me that love truly exists. He proved to me that I can be myself and I wouldn't be judged. He has proven to me that he can love me through sickness and in health. He has proven to me that he will love me through all my crazy episodes. No matter what, he will love me for all that I am and more. On this day, I married my soulmate.

# Ulcerative Colitis Warrior

I have ulcerative colitis. What is that? I wish I could tell you. Everyone is different, everyone is never the same. Our symptoms vary, no one is ever the same. We can change how we eat, we can take our meds, but the one thing we cannot do is forget the pain that exists. A pain that we sometimes hide, for we are afraid people might think we are faking it. This is a disease that is so invisible, that we all want to make it visible. I have ulcerative colitis, and I am a warrior and survivor.

# September 19, 2018

This is the day I gave birth to you. This is the day I said hello to you. This is the day I held your hand. This is the day that changed my life. This is the day I thank God I have you in my life now. For I will never be the same without you. You have given me the chance in a lifetime to love someone other than myself. I love you my sweet baby. You are an angel from God, and I thank him everyday for bringing you to me. I love you so much.

# Mother

My mother is the sweetest woman you could ever love. My mother has the kindest heart anyone could have. My mother has been there for me through thick and thin. However, mess with my mother and she will turn into a lioness. She will protect her cubs with all her might, for she is a strong woman. I thank her everyday for giving me the strength I thought I could never get. Without her love and support I would not be here today. So, thank you mother for everything you have done for me. I wish I could give you all that you want. Until then, this is all I can do.

# Autumn Leaf



Our little autumn leaf that fell from the heavens tree. You came into our lives at the moment we needed you the most. Here on Earth you are but a child, but in heaven you were a leaf waiting to be sent to me and your father. Little autumn leaf that fell from the heavens tree. Keep on guiding us now that you are here with us. Give us your love, give us your wisdom, give us everything so that we may do in return for you. You are loved. So be loved my little autumn leaf.

# Words of Wisdom

Even though things happen for a reason. Know it's for a purpose. Love is always complicated. Friendship is always insane. Remember you are always given a chance to think with your mind and your heart. Your heart always wins, while your mind always protects. Listen to them both. They will show you the way. They will guide you in the right direction. We as humans are always complicated. We as humans are always born with flaws. Sometimes we know what they are. Sometimes we don't. We all have a past. Whether we want to move beyond it is another thing. Our demons will always be with us, but that shouldn't stop us from loving those we care about. Know there are those who will always be there no matter what. Trust in your faith. Whatever that may be.

# Words of Wisdom 2

Even though times are hard, remember we all have each other. During this time of uncertainty, there are things we might need to reflect upon. I'm not sure what that might be, but I do know it needs to be done. We all are humans, we all have flaws. We all have strengths, and we all have weaknesses. This is the time to reflect, for we do not know when it is our time to leave this world. So whether we have bent up rage for someone, or we simply are angry with that person. Turn it around, talk to them, get over whatever resentment you have. For when you do, all will be will. This is a time to act. We mustn't be upset anymore. Remember, during this time of uncertainty there are things we might need to reflect upon. Take action. Or your time will forever be lost.

www.ingramcontent.com/pod-product-compliance
Lightning Source LLC
Chambersburg PA
CBHW070731160726
48003CB00006BA/2451